HOOT AND HOWL

ACROSS THE

DESERT

To my parents,
for my happy childhood in the desert.

To my daughter Pearl,
for asking so many inspiring questions.

VASSILIKI TZOMAKA

HOOT AND HOWL

ACROSS THE
DESERT

Life in the world's driest deserts

Thames & Hudson

CONTENTS

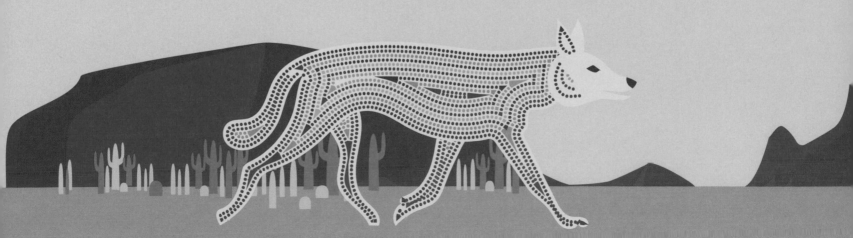

WHAT IS A DESERT?

Dry as a bone

A desert is a large area of land where very little rain falls. Deserts cover almost a third of the earth's surface. They can be divided into three main types – hot, cold or coastal. The most famous deserts are made of sand but many deserts are made of rock or even sheets of ice.

Water is essential to all life so animals and plants that live in deserts must adapt to the harsh, dry conditions. Over thousands of years, their bodies have developed special ways to survive with little or no water and in extremes of hot and cold.

Hot deserts

Hot deserts are found near the equator where the earth receives the most sunshine. Temperatures along the equator can reach as high as 50°C in the daytime but at night the heat escapes and the temperature can drop to below freezing. Wildlife in hot deserts must be able to survive extreme changes in temperature.

Coastal deserts

Coastal deserts are found where the land meets the ocean. Cold air from the ocean blows over the land and creates fog. This fog contains tiny droplets of water, which is the only water a coastal desert will receive. The plants and animals living in coastal deserts find different ways of collecting this water before it evaporates in the sun's heat.

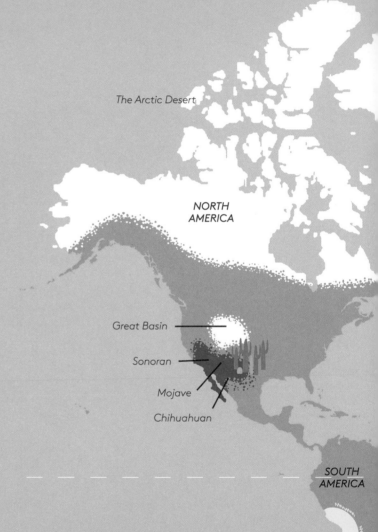

The Arctic Desert

NORTH AMERICA

Great Basin

Sonoran

Mojave

Chihuahuan

SOUTH AMERICA

Atacama

Patagonian

Cold deserts

The coldest deserts are the areas close to the North and South Poles. The poles don't receive any direct sunlight and spend six months of the year in darkness. The closer a desert is to the poles, the colder it is. Any water found in the air here freezes immediately and forms snow or ice. Animals in these deserts must survive the freezing winters or migrate to warmer places until the summer comes.

ARCTIC OCEAN

The Arctic Desert

EUROPE

ASIA

Gobi

ATLANTIC OCEAN

PACIFIC OCEAN

Arabian

Thar

Sahara

AFRICA

The Equator

INDIAN OCEAN

Namib

Kalahari

Great Victoria

Simpson

Great Sandy

Gibson

AUSTRALIA

Tanami

Hot deserts

Coastal deserts

Cold deserts

Other land

SOUTHERN OCEAN

ANTARCTICA

The Antarctic Desert

ROOTS AND RAIN
How do desert plants survive?

Plants that live in the desert are experts at finding and storing water. Some keep water in their leaves and others in their trunks. Others have very long roots that can reach water deep below the surface of the earth. For many animals living in the desert, plants are their only source of water.

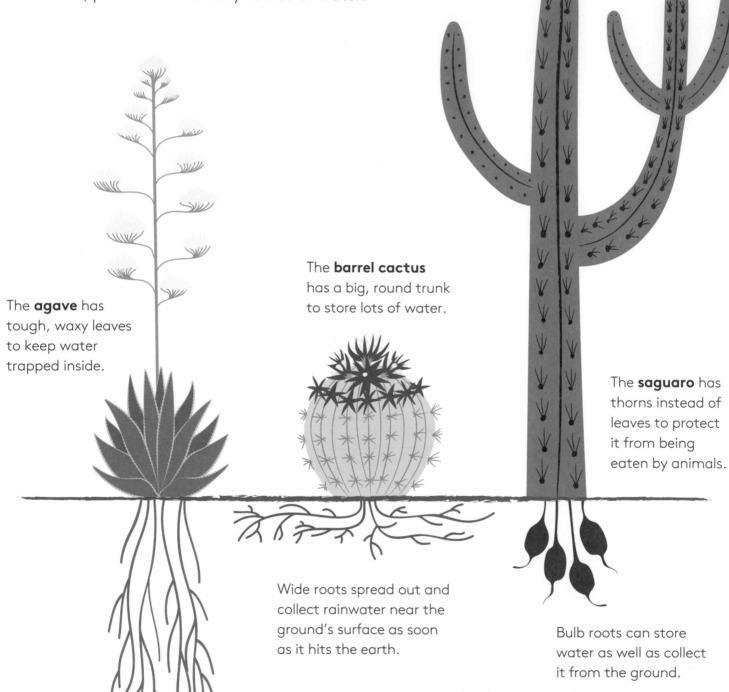

The **barrel cactus** has a big, round trunk to store lots of water.

The **agave** has tough, waxy leaves to keep water trapped inside.

The **saguaro** has thorns instead of leaves to protect it from being eaten by animals.

Wide roots spread out and collect rainwater near the ground's surface as soon as it hits the earth.

Bulb roots can store water as well as collect it from the ground.

Long roots collect water from deep underground springs.

How much water do we need to survive?

Humans need to drink 1-2 litres of water a day to keep our bodies working properly. In comparison, a cactus can survive for over a year without water.

How dry is a desert?

When a place receives less than 250 mm of rain in one year, it is dry enough to be called a desert. We know this because scientists have been measuring rainfall in different places around the world for hundreds of years. To do this, they use a rain-gauge, a device designed to trap and measure rainwater.

How much is one millimetre of rain?

One millimetre of rain means that one litre of rainwater has fallen over one square metre of land over the course of one hour.

Imagine standing in an area the size of your shower for an hour in light drizzle. That's how much water an entire desert receives every second day. It's not enough for a human to drink, let alone shower in! This is why desert wildlife must adapt in clever ways to survive.

Rainfall around the world

Every year, the American city of Seattle receives an average of 940 mm of rain. This is about seven and a half times more rain than the Sahara Desert, which gets an average of 125 mm in a year. Because deserts are such large areas, the amount of rainfall in a desert isn't the same across the entire desert. For example, some parts of the Sahara get less than 12 mm of rain every year, and others get up to 250 mm. This averages out at 125 mm in total.

New York, USA
1100 mm

Seattle, USA
940 mm

London,
UK
600 mm

Athens,
Greece 387 mm

Chihuahuan Desert
235 mm

Sahara Desert
125 mm

Antarctica
50 mm

ANTARCTICA
Freezing summers

Antarctica is the continent at the very bottom of the globe. It is the largest desert in the world and the coldest place on Earth. Very few animals live in Antarctica during the winter, when temperatures can be as low as –80°C. In the summer, when the long hours of sunshine melt some of the snow, animals that have adapted to living in cold conditions migrate to the Antarctic coast.

The **snow petrel** lives on the shores of Antarctica all year round.

During warm summers, the **chinstrap penguin** sometimes visits Antarctica.

In the summer, thousands of **Adelie penguins** arrive to lay their eggs. They make nests out of rocks and pebbles along the shore where the snow has melted.

Emperor penguins are the largest of all penguins and can grow to more than 120 cm tall.

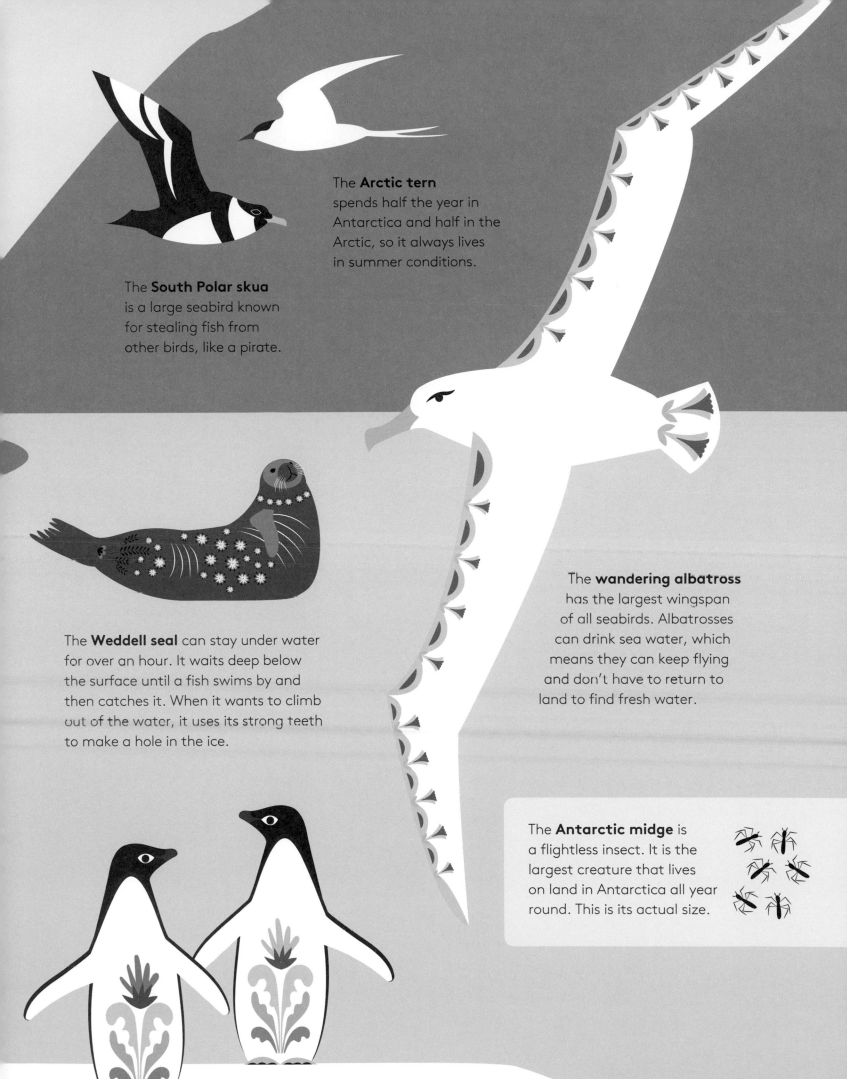

The **Arctic tern**
spends half the year in
Antarctica and half in the
Arctic, so it always lives
in summer conditions.

The **South Polar skua**
is a large seabird known
for stealing fish from
other birds, like a pirate.

The **Weddell seal** can stay under water
for over an hour. It waits deep below
the surface until a fish swims by and
then catches it. When it wants to climb
out of the water, it uses its strong teeth
to make a hole in the ice.

The **wandering albatross**
has the largest wingspan
of all seabirds. Albatrosses
can drink sea water, which
means they can keep flying
and don't have to return to
land to find fresh water.

The **Antarctic midge** is
a flightless insect. It is the
largest creature that lives
on land in Antarctica all year
round. This is its actual size.

THE ARCTIC
Wrapped up warm

Like Antarctica, the Arctic is a freezing cold desert but because it isn't quite as cold, it is home to many more animals.

Animals that live here store lots of body fat or grow thick coats to keep warm. In the winter, many Arctic animals grow white coats so that they can hide from predators in the snow.

The **snowy owl** hunts both by day and by night, unlike other owls that hunt mainly in the dark.

A **polar bear** can weigh up to 750 kg. Its fur has no colour, but when it reflects the light of the sun, it looks white. Underneath its fur, its skin is black!

The **walrus** spends as much time in the sea as it does on land. It uses its sensitive whiskers to find food.

TUNDRA

Tundra is the name given to land where it is too cold for trees to grow. In the Arctic tundra, low and bushy plants grow in summer when the sun melts the icy ground. The plants include **Arctic poppies** (1), **Arctic willow** (2), **cotton grass** (3) and **bear berries** (4). Lots of animals like to eat them.

The **Arctic squirrel** goes into a deep sleep during winter.

Different types of **reindeer** can be recognised by the shapes of their antlers. This one is a **Peary caribou**.

Arctic hares huddle together to keep warm in winter.

The **Arctic wolf** is an excellent swimmer and can hunt across both land and sea.

A **weasel** preys on other animals such as lemmings. It is small so that it can follow them into burrows.

The **Arctic fox** can smell and hear incredibly well. When it senses something moving under the snow, it jumps up high and then crashes down to break through the surface.

Lemmings live in underground colonies with lots of rooms.

13

THE GREAT BASIN
A natural bowl

Made up almost entirely of scrubland, the Great Basin is the largest desert in North America. It is called the Great Basin because the mountains surrounding it give it a basin shape!

Sagebrush covers the plains of the Great Basin and is a major source of food for the animals that live here. It also makes a good hiding place for smaller animals that want to avoid hungry pumas that come down from the mountains.

The **pronghorn** is the second fastest land animal in the world, after the cheetah. Its powerful legs help it spring across the plains to escape from predators, such as the coyote.

The **greater sage-grouse** uses the sagebrush for food and shelter all year round. In the spring, the male sage-grouse puffs out the yellow balloons on its chest and dances to attract a female.

The **Utah prairie dog** lives in burrows under the grasslands. If it senses any predators nearby, it whistles to warn its family.

The **Ancient Bristlecone Pine Forest** is part of the Great Basin. It is home to some of the oldest trees in the world. These trees can shut down some of their branches and parts of their trunks so they don't need as much water.

The location of the oldest **bristlecone pine** in the forest is kept secret to help protect it from getting too many human visitors. It is believed to be about 5,000 years old.

Chipmunks like to run along the branches of these ancient trees looking for food. They fill their cheek pouches with as many seeds as they can and carry them home to their burrows.

THE SONORAN DESERT
Turning up the heat

The hot Sonoran Desert is packed full of many types of prickly cactus. The cacti and their fruit and flowers attract all sorts of insects, birds and animals that need the plants to survive.

Gila woodpeckers peck holes called 'boots' into the sides of the saguaro cactus to make safe nests. As soon as their babies learn to fly, they abandon their nest.

Barrel cacti get their name from their shape.

When it wants to nest and lay eggs, the **elf owl** moves into a 'boot' abandoned by Gila woodpeckers. It is the smallest owl in the world, measuring only 12–14 cm high.

The stem of the **saguaro cactus** is covered with spikes to protect it from being eaten by animals. Like other cacti, it grows flowers and sweet fruit.

When **Harris's antelope squirrels** get hot, they find a shady spot and spread out their bodies to cool down. This is called heat dumping. When they can't find any shade, they use their big tails to make shade for themselves.

Coyotes hunt alone or in packs and will eat anything, including prickly pear fruit, flowers and insects, such as the **many-hued grasshopper**. They talk to each other by howling.

ANNA'S HUMMINGBIRD
Small but spectacular

Anna's hummingbirds are native to the Sonoran Desert. Like other hummingbirds, they are excellent fliers, and despite their tiny size, they can survive even the most challenging desert conditions.

A male Anna's hummingbird is easy to spot because it has feathers on its head and throat that change from green to pink in the sunlight.

Hummingbirds move their wings in the shape of a figure of eight. This allows them to fly forwards, backwards, up and down, and even upside down.

Hummingbirds need a lot of energy, which they get by drinking the nectar of flowers. Because they can flap their wings up to 90 times a second, they can hover in mid-air to feed from flowers, instead of landing.

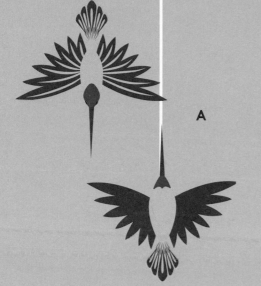

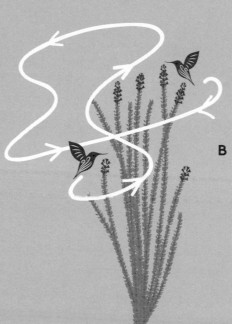

A

B

FLIGHT PATHS

When males want to show off, they put on a dive display. They fly as high as 35 m up in the air and zoom down towards the ground before swooping up again.

A: Rocketing up and plummeting down
B: Zigzagging around a vine cactus
C: Looping around a clump of saguaro cacti

C

TONGUE TWISTER

Hummingbirds have a special way of drinking. They have a very long tongue that starts at the top of their head, curls right around the back, under their chin and out through their beak. It's also forked so it can lap up nectar twice as fast.

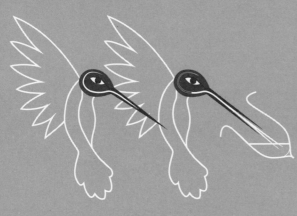

THE CHIHUAHUAN & MOJAVE DESERTS
Toughing it out

The Mojave Desert is the driest of the North American deserts, receiving less than 120 mm of rainfall a year. Only true desert animals can survive in such hot and dry conditions. The nearby Chihuahuan Desert is the largest of the hot North American deserts and is home to a huge variety of plants and animals.

The **prickly pear cactus** is very popular with hungry and thirsty animals. Its leaves and fruit are good to eat and full of water and its sharp spikes are easy to remove.

Collared peccaries like to live in large family groups. They search for food, such as prickly pear fruit, by day and by night.

The **antelope jackrabbit** uses its enormous ears to keep itself cool in the heat.

The **roadrunner** runs so fast that its feet don't touch the ground long enough to get hot.

The **ringtail** is an excellent climber. In the daytime, it sleeps in the leafy shade of the **Joshua tree**.

When **bighorn sheep** and **mule deer** are thirsty and there's no water nearby, they use their horns or hooves to knock the spines out of cacti, so they can eat the juicy flesh.

The **pipevine swallowtail butterfly** lays its eggs on the **Dutchman's pipevine**. Its caterpillars store the poison from the plant in their bodies. This makes them poisonous to any animal that might want to eat them!

The **clouded yellow butterfly** lives in the **palo verde tree**. It hides from predators among the yellow flowers.

The **Dutchman's pipevine** is poisonous to most animals and insects. This is the vine's way of stopping animals from eating it.

NOCTURNAL ANIMALS
Night-time superpowers

As the sun starts to set, the Earth begins to cool down and animals that have been hiding from the heat of the day start to wake up. They have a lot to do before the sun rises and it gets too hot again. These animals have special ways of finding food and keeping safe from predators in the dark.

The **kangaroo rat** only comes out at night to hunt for food. It has excellent hearing and can jump as high as 2.75 m to escape from danger.

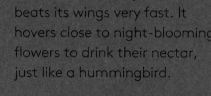

The **white-lined sphinx moth** beats its wings very fast. It hovers close to night-blooming flowers to drink their nectar, just like a hummingbird.

The **puma** likes to live in caves that provide shelter from the heat of the day. It comes out to hunt at dawn and dusk.

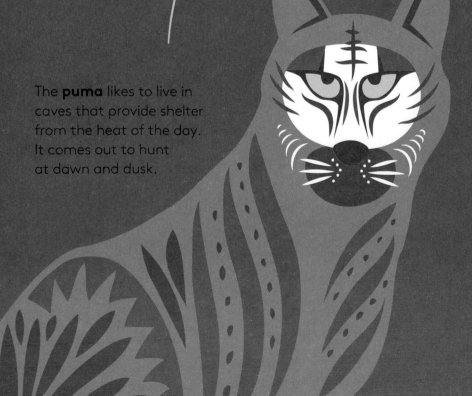

The **great horned owl** has soft wings so that it can fly very quietly. It sneaks up on small animals like snakes, mice and rabbits.

The **lesser long-nosed bat** uses its very long tongue to reach the nectar hidden deep inside desert flowers, like the blooms of the **saguaro cactus**.

The **porcupine** has sharp spines called quills to protect itself from predators. If a bigger animal attacks, the quills will get stuck in its skin. The quills are covered with tiny barbs, so they are hard to pull out.

23

THE ATACAMA DESERT
Dry as can be

Parts of the Atacama Desert have not had any rain for over 15 million years. Few animals and birds live in this coastal desert. In some areas, salt lakes have formed. Most of the wildlife in the Atacama is found near the salt lakes as it is easier to find food there.

Chilean and Andean flamingos get their pink colours from the food that they eat. Their beaks have fringed edges that work like a sieve, helping them to filter tiny creatures out of the salty water.

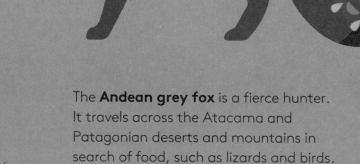

The **Andean grey fox** is a fierce hunter. It travels across the Atacama and Patagonian deserts and mountains in search of food, such as lizards and birds.

The **southern viscacha** is a furry rodent that looks like a rabbit with a squirrel's tail. It likes to sunbathe on rocks in the daytime and searches for plants to eat at dawn and dusk.

The **Andes** run along the edge of the Atacama Desert. These massive mountains form a barrier that stops clouds from reaching the desert, so very little rain falls.

The **vicuña** is the wild relative of the alpaca. This very shy animal has excellent hearing and very soft fur to keep warm. It drinks salt water and eats any grass it can find to survive.

The **Andean mountain cat** has a very long, thick tail. It uses it to balance when hunting on steep mountain slopes and to keep itself warm.

Plants such as **yareta** and **pussypaws** sometimes bloom in the coastal desert.

THE PATAGONIAN DESERT
A long way to run

Between the Andes in Argentina and the Atlantic Ocean is the cold Patagonian Desert. It is the largest desert in South America.

Animals that live here must be able to run fast to escape from predators. On the flat grassy plains, there are very few places to hide.

Condors don't build proper nests. They lay their eggs on high cliff ledges with a few twigs around them.

The **Andean condor** has black velvety feathers like a cape and a bald head, sometimes with a comb on top, that can change colour depending on its mood.

It flies from the Atacama Desert to the Patagonian Desert in search of food and it prefers to eat animals that are already dead. This kind of dead meat is called carrion.

Female condors have red eyes and no comb on the top of their head.

ESCAPING PREDATORS
Keeping out of trouble

The animals that live in the Patagonian Desert have special ways to escape predators. Small animals use their claws to dig burrows to hide in. Larger animals have long legs to run away from anything that chases them.

The **guanaco** is a wild llama. It is an excellent runner and likes to hang out in big groups.

Darwin's rhea is a large bird that doesn't fly. Its strong legs help it run very, very fast and its thick feathers help to keep it warm.

The **burrowing owl** has the longest legs of all owls and prefers to walk rather than fly. It lives in underground burrows.

The **mara** is a very large rodent. It has long powerful legs, which help it run away from predators.

The **tuco tuco** is a small furry rodent. It gets its name from the sound it makes when it digs its burrow, where it spends most of its time.

The **pichi** is a type of small armadillo. Its back is covered in leathery armour. When threatened, it lies flat on the ground to protect its soft belly.

THE NAMIB DESERT
High and mighty

Lying on the coast of southern Africa, the Namib Desert is 55 million years old. It is the oldest desert in the world. Winds blowing in from the ocean create its high sand dunes and bring with them tiny droplets of water. Lots of the plants and animals that live here find clever ways of collecting this water in order to survive.

The **black-backed jackal** eats insects and chameleons. Its fox-like colours help it hide in the red sand of the Namib dunes.

The **springbok** can spend its entire life without drinking any water. It gets all the water it needs from the juicy plants that it eats.

The **Namaqua chameleon** changes colour to help control its body temperature. In the morning, it turns dark to soak up the warmth from the sun. By midday, it turns white to reflect the sun's fierce heat.

Fog that moves across the desert leaves water droplets on rocks. Thirsty animals lick the water off the rocks.

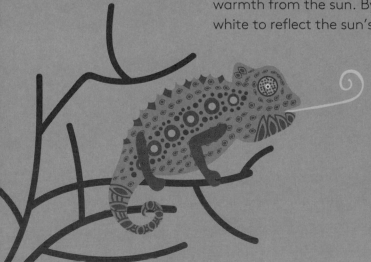

These **camel thorn trees** died hundreds of years ago because there wasn't enough water for them. The dead trees have been preserved by the dry climate and burned black by the scorching rays of the sun.

The **gemsbok** can survive for weeks without water. Its white belly reflects back the heat from the ground, helping it to keep cool.

The **wheel spider** moves quickly by doing cartwheels and dives into the sand to hide.

The **darkling beetle** lifts up its body to catch fog on the bumps on its back. As the fog turns into water, the drops slide down into the beetle's mouth.

The **welwitschia** plant absorbs most of its water from fog in the air and dew on the ground. Antelopes like to eat the soft parts of the stem to get at the water inside.

29

THE KALAHARI DESERT
Hunger games

Spread across Namibia, Botswana and South Africa, the Kalahari Desert is an unusual desert because it occasionally rains here.

Watering holes form where the soil is less sandy and the water can't drain away as easily. These watering holes attract many animals – some fiercer than others. Prey animals must watch out and stay on the move to survive on these grassy savannah plains.

The **leopard** is excellent at climbing trees. It rests in their branches to keep cool in the heat of the day.

The **Kalahari lion** has the biggest paws and slimmest body of all lions. It can walk long distances and survive without water for up to two weeks.

The **cheetah** is the fastest land animal in the world. It can kill a small animal like a hare with just one bite.

An **African elephant** can use its feet to sense rain coming from a long way away. After it visits a watering hole, it will always remember the quickest way back there.

The **black rhinoceros**, is one of the last five species of rhinos left in the world. It uses its horns to protect itself.

The **blue wildebeest** stamps its feet and runs fast in large groups to escape its enemies.

Zebras stick together in groups called herds. If a zebra is attacked, its family will come to protect it, surrounding the wounded zebra and trying to drive predators away.

ACACIA TREES
Treetop neighbourhood

Acacia trees are found in all African deserts and are especially common in the Kalahari. They are tall and hardy and their leafy branches provide a shady haven for the desert's wildlife.

FAVOURITE FOOD

With its very long, tough black tongue, a giraffe can eat the thorny acacia branches without hurting itself.

When a giraffe eats too many leaves from one tree, the acacia starts to grow leaves only on the branches that are too high for giraffes to reach.

It also lets off a special smell that drifts to other trees. This acts as a signal that giraffes could soon be heading their way.

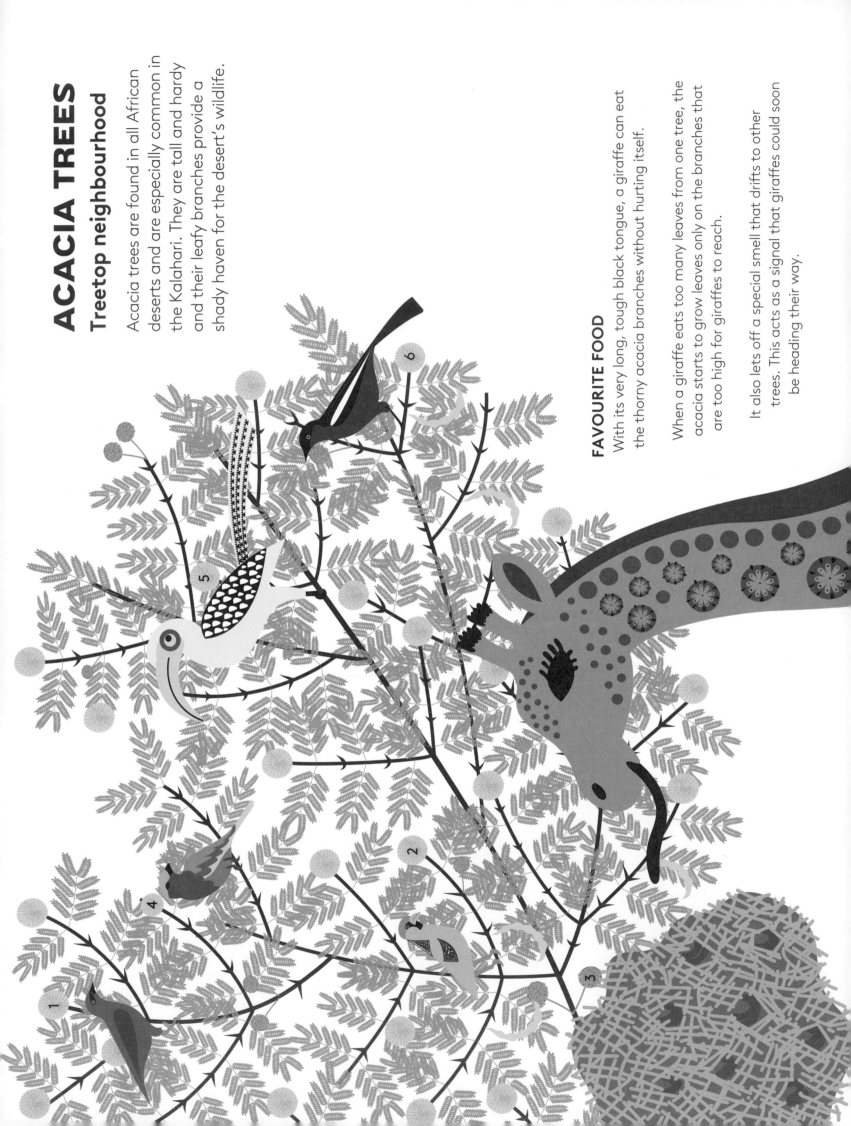

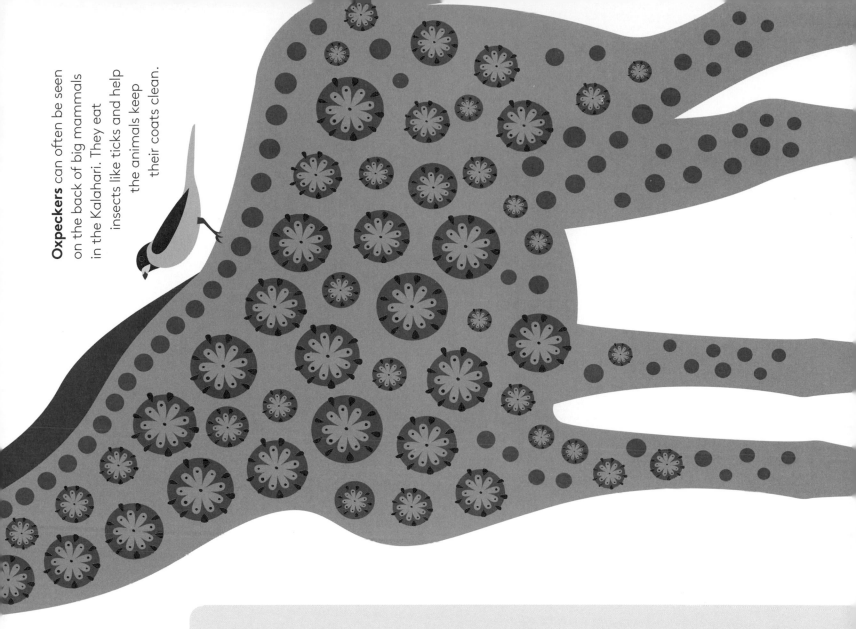

Oxpeckers can often be seen on the back of big mammals in the Kalahari. They eat insects like ticks and help the animals keep their coats clean.

BIRD CITIES

Many birds like to shelter in the leafy branches of the acacia. Some make nests for their families and others perch on the branches while searching for food.

African starlings (1) make small neighbourhoods in acacias and raise their young together. This is important because it means parents can take turns to search for food.

Sociable weavers (2) work together to make enormous nests (**3**). With separate sections for each family, one nest can be a home for up to 300 birds.

The **lilac-breasted roller (4)** prefers to make its nest in empty holes in baobab trees. It likes to perch on acacia branches while looking for insects to eat.

The **southern yellow-billed hornbill (5)** likes to sleep on the highest branches where it is safe from larger predators.

The **crimson-breasted shrike (6)** spends its days looking for ants and other insects to eat by walking around on the ground underneath the tree.

THE SAHARA
Keeping cool as a cucumber

The Sahara receives more sunshine than any other part of the world and covers most of North Africa.

The long hours of sunshine mean the sand gets extremely hot during the day. Animals that live here have to be able to survive the heat and lack of shade, and cope with the very hot sand!

The **dromedary camel** can live for more than a week without water. To cool itself down, it pees on its own legs. This makes it very smelly!

The **addax** grows a white coat in summer to reflect the sun's heat. In winter, its coat turns brown.

A **bitter cucumber** is a wild version of a watermelon plant. Its fruits are poisonous to eat.

The shiny **dung beetle** collects dung and rolls it into a round ball. It uses the ball as a place to rest when it wants to cool off from the heat of the sand.

The **dorcas gazelle** spends the hottest parts of the day in the shade. It pants through its nose when it needs to cool down.

The **fennec fox** is the world's smallest fox. Its big ears give off body heat and help it to stay cool.

An **ostrich** has huge, wide toes so it can walk across the sand without sinking in.

The **Saharan silver ant** has long legs to lift its body off the hot sand. Its back is covered with special hairs that reflect the sun's heat. This means it can come out to look for food at the hottest time of the day.

West African crocodiles sleep through the driest months of the year in caves and burrows but will gather near an oasis when it is full of water.

The **crimson-speckled moth** has red and black spotted wings to warn predators that it is poisonous. It likes to feed on the flowers of the **desert heliotrope**.

A DESERT OASIS
Slice of paradise

In some parts of the Saharan desert, underground water sources come to the surface to form freshwater pools. Date palms and bushes grow around these pools, forming what is known as an oasis. An oasis provides food and shelter for animals but it is not always safe to stay for a long time. Large predators may also visit the oasis to hunt for their next meal.

The **Rüppell's weaver bird** weaves beautiful nests that dangle from the branches of palm trees like Christmas baubles.

Desert locusts can fly hundreds of kilometres in a day, using the wind to help them. They form huge cloud-like swarms that can contain millions of locusts. Because they breed so quickly and eat so much, locust swarms can cause famines for animals and humans.

THE ARABIAN DESERT
Nothing but sand for miles

The Arabian Desert is the fifth largest desert in the world. In its centre is the Empty Quarter, the largest expanse of sand in the world.

There are very few plants here, so animals spend their time moving from one oasis to another to find food and water. Some live in the mountains surrounding the desert and never go out into the sand dunes where there is little protection from danger.

The **golden jackal** can survive without water for long periods of time and will eat almost anything.

The **honey badger** is a fearless animal. It has loose skin on the back of its neck so that it can twist its head around to bite an attacker.

The **desert hedgehog** curls up into a small spiky ball to protect itself from predators such as the sand cat.

The **sand cat** has large fluffy paws, which help it walk across hot sand without sinking in.

The **peregrine falcon** is an excellent hunter, due to its fast speed and sharp eyesight.

The **Arabian oryx** uses its very long horns to protect itself from predators, including the jackal.

Hamadryas baboons prefer mountain areas where there is more water. They live in troops of up to 300 members. Their pink, padded bottoms make it more comfortable to sit on rocks or hard ground.

A **camel spider** is a fierce hunter. Its large, powerful pincers help it to capture prey much bigger than itself such as lizards, birds and rodents.

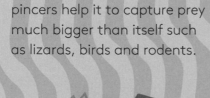

SAND DUNES
Gone with the wind

Although there is very little rain over sandy deserts, there is often plenty of wind. As the wind blows over the sand, it lifts the lightest grains and moves them along in a series of leaps and hops. This is called saltation. This process makes sand dunes move over time.

Saltation

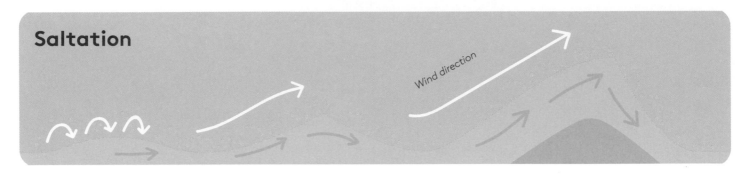

Wind direction

Sand dune shapes

The shape of a sand dune depends on wind speed, wind direction and how much sand there is. Here is a bird's eye view of six different sand dune patterns. The white arrows show the direction of the wind.

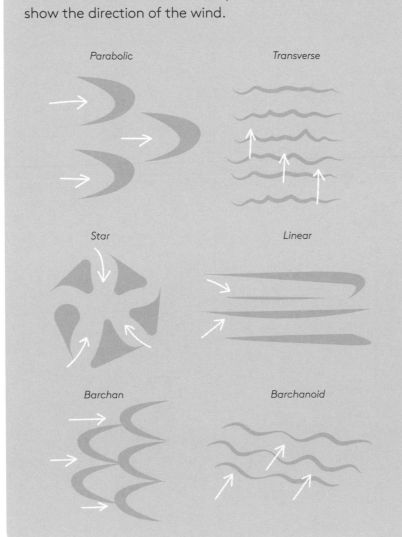

Parabolic

Transverse

Star

Linear

Barchan

Barchanoid

Sandstorms

A sandstorm cloud

Strong winds can move lots of grains of sand in one go, causing sandstorms. Sometimes, after very windy weather, the landscape can look completely different from one day to the next.

Sand ripples

The direction of the wind can also be seen in the ripples in the sand.

DESERT LIZARDS
Cold-blooded creatures

Lizards are cold-blooded, which means they rely on their environment to help warm their bodies. This is why many lizards are found in deserts where they can bask in the sun's heat. There are over 6,000 types of lizards in the world.

The **horned desert lizard** puffs up its body and squirts blood from its eyes when it wants to look scary!

The **thorny devil** lives in the Australian deserts. It uses its spikes for camouflage and protection.

The **zebra-tailed lizard** lives mainly in the Mojave and Great Basin as it doesn't like to get too hot.

The **desert iguana** can run around at the hottest times of day without getting too hot.

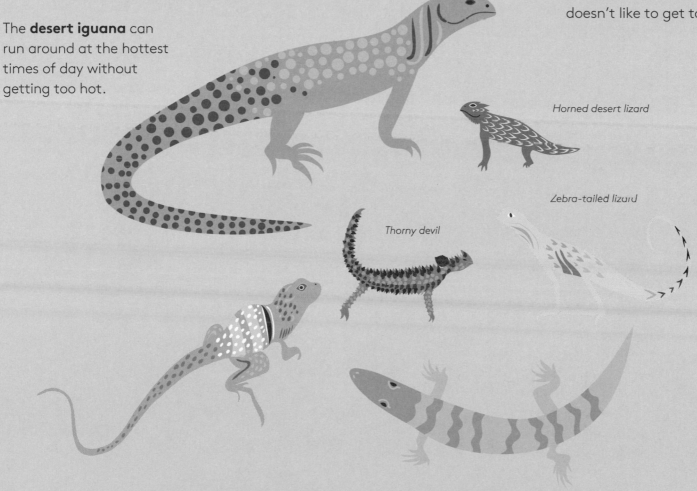

Horned desert lizard

Zebra-tailed lizard

Thorny devil

The **collared lizard** lives in the hot North American deserts. It can run very fast on only its back legs.

The **great desert skink** is found in Australia. Skinks can 'swim' in the sand and are the only lizards that live in communities.

THE THAR DESERT
Small wonder

The small Thar Desert lies between India and Pakistan. Even though more humans live here than in any other desert in the world, it is still truly wild.

The Thar is a hot sandy desert and has a lot of wildlife in common with the African and Arabian deserts. However, there are some plants and animals that are only found in this area.

The **khejri tree** is found in many Arabian deserts as well as the Thar. It provides food and shelter for both animals and humans.

The **Indian wild ass** is one of the fastest animals in India. Its speed helps it to cover large areas when searching for food and water.

The **great Indian bustard** is a very rare bird. Males have a pouch under their bill, which they blow up like a balloon to attract females. It also makes their calls louder.

The **desert teak tree** grows in the Thar. Its beautiful bright red flowers are often eaten by passing camels.

The **Indian peacock** displays its beautiful feathers when it wants to attract a female, called a peahen. It also does this to look big and powerful when it needs to scare off predators.

The **Indian spiny-tailed lizard** is a large lizard native to the Thar Desert. It is hunted by many animals for its fat, spiky tail that makes a tasty meal.

WILD BACTRIAN CAMEL
Ships of the desert

When you think of a camel, you might think of hot deserts, but the wild Bactrian camel lives in the colder deserts of Asia. To cope with cold winters and hot summers, Bactrian camels grow a thick, shaggy coat in winter that falls out during the warmer summer months.

Although there are millions of camels all over the world, the **wild Bactrian camel** is in danger of extinction. Less than 1,000 live in the Gobi Desert today.

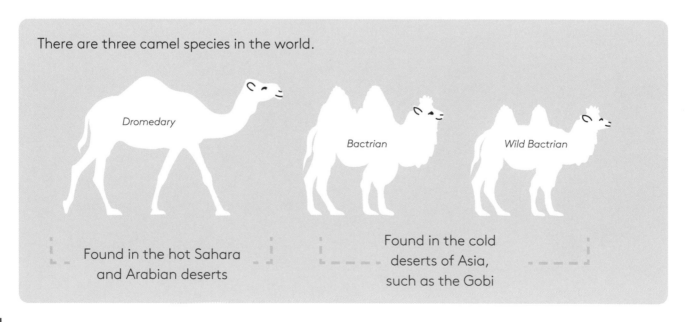

There are three camel species in the world.

Dromedary

Bactrian

Wild Bactrian

Found in the hot Sahara and Arabian deserts

Found in the cold deserts of Asia, such as the Gobi

DESERT PROTECTION

Camels have evolved to live in the desert over millions of years. They have developed special ways of dealing with the heat, the sand and the lack of water. Because of this, they have helped humans to cross the deserts of Africa and Asia for centuries.

Three eyelids and two rows of eyelashes to protect and clean their eyes during sandstorms.

Hairy ears to stop sand from getting in.

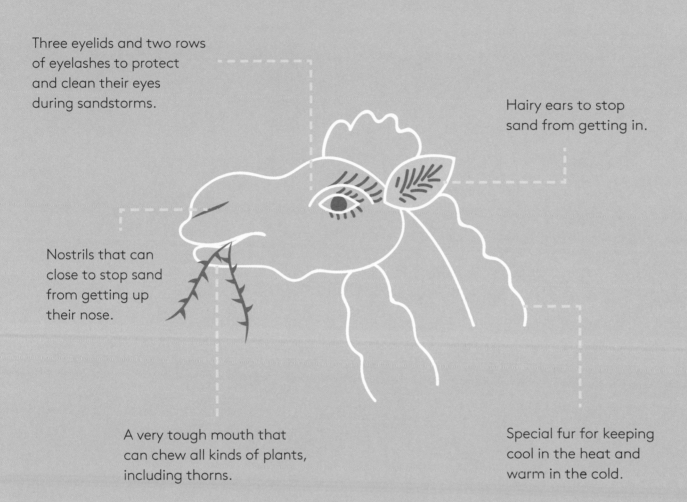

Nostrils that can close to stop sand from getting up their nose.

A very tough mouth that can chew all kinds of plants, including thorns.

Special fur for keeping cool in the heat and warm in the cold.

THE FASTEST DRINKERS

A very thirsty camel can drink a whole bathtub of water in 15 minutes.

THE GOBI DESERT
A safe haven

The Gobi is the largest desert in Asia, covering large parts of China and Mongolia.

It is very cold in the winter and very hot in the summer. Life is tough here, even for animals who are able to survive the extreme conditions.

The **Pallas's fish eagle** uses the marshes as its breeding ground.

The **wild Bactrian camel** eats snow when there is no water.

Przewalski's horses live in the wild in small family groups and use sounds, scents, and ear and body positions to communicate.

The spots on the **snow leopard's** coat act as camouflage on the rocky slopes. Unfortunately it is hunted by humans for its beautifully patterned fur.

One of the largest nature reserves in the world has been created in the south of the Gobi Desert to protect endangered species. Here animals can live away from human dangers like hunting and the land is protected from farming.

The **saiga** is a type of antelope. It has a strangely shaped nose to help to keep out the dust during dry summers.

Less than 40 **Gobi bears** are left in the world today. They live in a protected part of Mongolia where they can eat wild rhubarb, their favourite food.

THE AUSTRALIAN DESERTS
It's all Outback

Almost a third of Australia is made up of deserts. These deserts are mainly found in the middle of the country, an area known as the Outback. The largest ones are the Great Victoria Desert, the Great Sandy Desert, the Tanami Desert, the Simpson Desert and the Gibson Desert. Large sandstone formations can be seen in some places in the Australian deserts, making it easier to find your way.

Kangaroos and wallabies are marsupials. This means they carry their babies in a pouch. The **red kangaroo** is the largest of all kangaroos. It can jump as far as 9 m in one leap. This helps it travel long distances across the desert, searching for grass to eat.

The Pinnacles

The **emu**'s long neck allows it to spot predators over the tallest grasses.

A baby kangaroo is called a **joey**.

The **perentie** is the biggest lizard in Australia and can grow to 2.5 m long. It is hard to spot because it burrows into the ground by digging with its powerful front legs and strong claws.

The **galah cockatoo** is easy to spot with its bright pink head and chest. It likes to live in **eucalyptus trees** that grow in the Australian deserts. It will dance along a branch to get the attention of a mate.

Kata Tjuta Rocks

Uluru, also known as Ayers Rock

The **bilby** digs long tunnels among the **spinifex** bushes to shelter from the heat and from predators.

The **dingo** is a wild dog. It usually hunts small animals like rabbits, lizards and birds but sometimes it catches big animals like kangaroos.

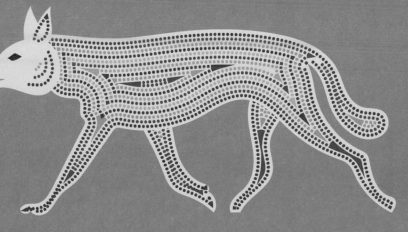

The **warru** is a shy rock wallaby. It hides in rocky caves to escape the heat of the day and comes out at night.

The **burrowing frog** spends most of its life underground. It only comes out when it rains, which does not happen often!

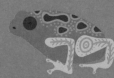

VENOMOUS ANIMALS
Danger in the desert

Some desert animals, such as snakes or scorpions, are venomous. Venom is a poison that is injected by a bite or a sting. Animals use venom to attack their prey, or to defend themselves against predators. They store it in their bodies in little pockets called venom sacs.

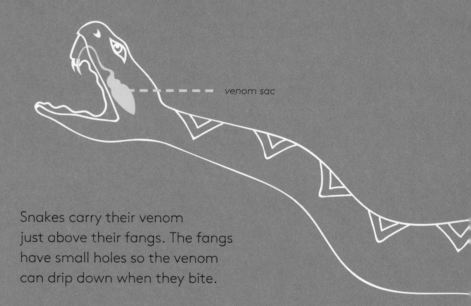

venom sac

The **black widow spider** lives in the hot deserts of North America. It has two venom-filled fangs at the front of its head.

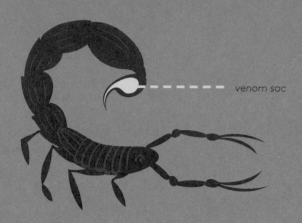

venom sac

The **deathstalker scorpion** is one of the most dangerous scorpions in the world and can be found in the Sahara and Arabian Deserts. It carries its venom in its tail.

venom sac

Snakes carry their venom just above their fangs. The fangs have small holes so the venom can drip down when they bite.

Desert monitor lizard

venom sacs

Gila monster lizard

Not many desert lizards are venomous. The ones that are carry their venom under their tongues. They pass it onto their victim through their saliva when they bite.

DESERT SNAKES
Seriously scaly

Snakes, just like lizards, are cold-blooded reptiles. They are found in all deserts except the Arctic and Antarctica but they are most common in hot deserts, where they come out at night when the earth is cooler.

The **desert horned viper** lives in the Sahara and Arabian Deserts. It hides in the sand and leaves a wavy shape behind it when it moves. Its venom contains 13 kinds of toxins and can cause serious illness.

*Desert horned viper
30–60 cm long*

The **western diamondback rattlesnake** is found in the hot American deserts. Its tail makes a rattling sound as a warning. It is quick to attack and can jump quite a long way.

*Saw-scaled viper
90 cm long*

*Western diamondback rattlesnake
120 cm long*

The **saw-scaled viper** is found in Africa and the Middle East. It curves into a U-shape when it's resting. As a warning, it rubs its scales together to make a sizzling sound.

The **inland taipan** lives in the Australian deserts. It is a shy snake that can be found in rocky areas. Its venom is the deadliest in the world and can kill a human in just 30 minutes.

*Inland taipan
180 cm long*

DESERT FOLK ART
Patterns by people

To survive the tough conditions, the people that live in and around deserts sometimes follow a nomadic way of life. Nomads move from place to place in search of water, food and shelter, and rely on what nature provides for most of their needs. The illustrations in this book are inspired by the colours and patterns found in the folk art of desert communities.

Geometric patterns
Many Native American artists have traditionally used geometric shapes to make patterns. They are often woven into fabrics and baskets.

Alebrijes
Sculptures called *alebrijes* are a part of Mexican folk art. They are made from carved wood or papier mâché and are known for their exaggerated features and bold imaginative colours.

Inuit patterns

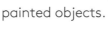

Inuit tribes who live in or near the Arctic create patterns from lines. They are used to decorate knitted, carved or painted objects.

Floral patterns

Middle Eastern and Asian patterns are often inspired by nature. Leaves, swirls and flowers are used to decorate woven goods made by the people that live in these deserts.

African patterns

African tribes make accessories and jewellery from beads and carved wood, decorated with repeated lines, circles and dots.

Aboriginal patterns

Indigenous Australian artists use patterns made up of painted or carved dots and circles to decorate their belongings. These symbols often represent the relationship between humans and nature.

53

GLOSSARY

ENDANGERED – an animal or plant that is dying out and soon may not exist anymore.

EQUATOR – an imaginary line that divides the Earth into two halves, called hemispheres.

EVAPORATION – the process by which a liquid turns into a gas.

EXTINCT – an animal is extinct when no more members of its species are alive.

MIGRATE – when birds or animals travel to another place at the same time every year.

NATIVE – a plant or animal that lives naturally in a particular place and hasn't been introduced from somewhere else.

NOCTURNAL – an animal that moves around and feeds at night.

PREDATOR – an animal that hunts and kills other animals for food.

PREY – an animal that is hunted or caught by other animals for food.

REPTILE – a cold-blooded animal that lays eggs and is covered in scales or plates.

VENOM – a poisonous substance made inside the bodies of animals such as snakes, spiders, and scorpions, injected by a bite or a sting.

INDEX

First published in the United Kingdom in 2020 by
Thames & Hudson Ltd, 181A High Holborn, London WC1V 7QX

Hoot and Howl Across the Desert © 2020 Vassiliki Tzomaka

Consultancy by Barbara Taylor

British Library Cataloguing-in-Publication Data
A catalogue record for this book is available from the British Library

ISBN 978-0-500-65198-8

Printed and bound in China by Leo Paper Products Ltd.

To find out about all our publications, please visit
www.thamesandhudson.com. There you can subscribe
to our e-newsletter, browse or download our current
catalogue, and buy any titles that are in print.

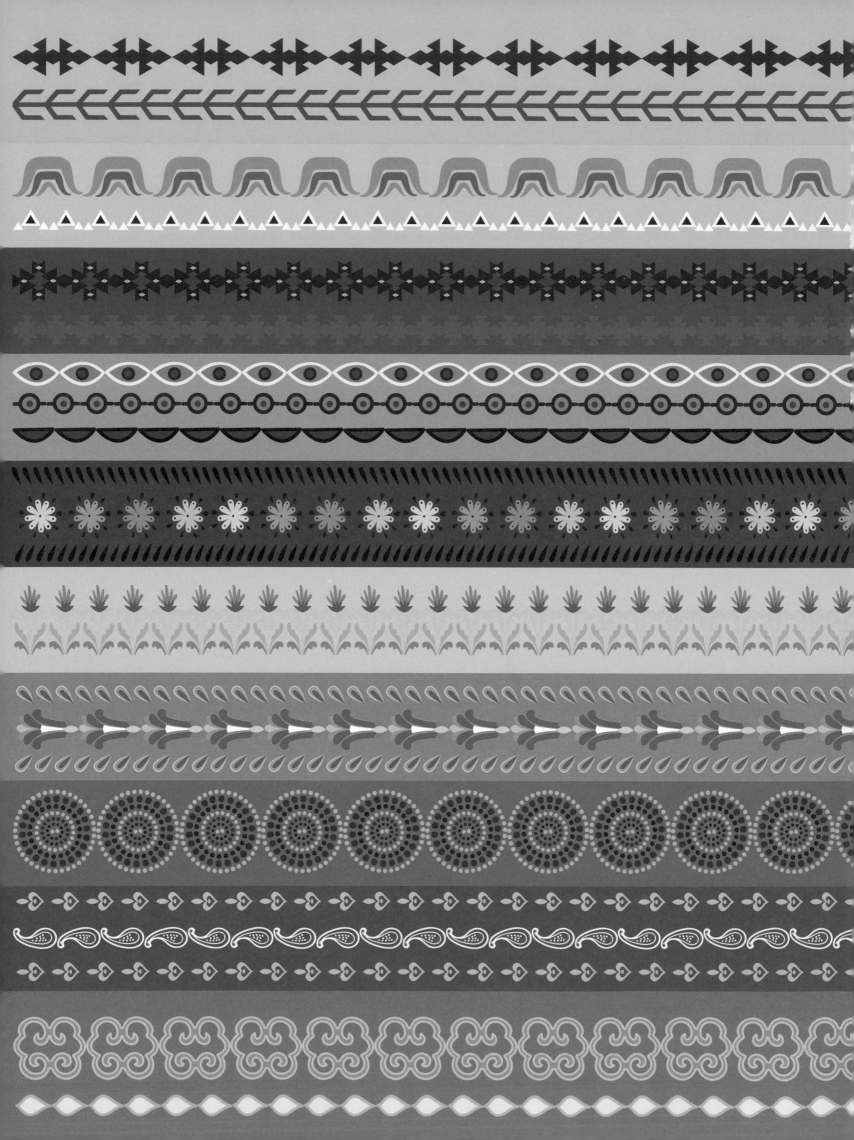